Tuesday
1:30

THE GUIDED
dream
journal

THE GUIDED
dream
journal

Record, Reflect, and Interpret
the Hidden Meanings in Your Dreams

KATHERINE OLIVETTI

ROCKRIDGE
PRESS

Interior and Cover Designer: Stephanie Sumulong
Art Producer: Michael Hardgrove
Editor: Emily Angell
Production Editor: Ashley Polikoff
Photography: Author photo courtesy of © Peter Olivetti
Illustrations: © SNIPESCIENTIST/Creative Market
ISBN: Print 978-1-64611-875-5 | eBook 978-1-64611-876-2

R0

THIS JOURNAL BELONGS TO

_____

contents

THE
DREAM IS
A LITTLE
HIDDEN DOOR
IN THE
INNERMOST
AND MOST
SECRET
RECESSES
OF
THE SOUL.

—C. G. JUNG

Introduction

Beginning in my childhood, first thing in the morning after waking, I'd lie in bed and try to remember the dream I had during the night. Whether it was entertaining, terrifying, haunting, mystifying, or delightfully reality-defying, every dream captured my interest. The idea that it was possible to be sound asleep, my mind and body resting, while some part of me was busily inventing images, stories, characters, and even depicting people, places, and things that never existed, intrigued me. It did then and still does today. Even as a youngster I had an awareness—not only of being the character in the dream but also of the experience of dreaming—so that even during a nightmare, while one part of me was terrified and woke shaking and sweaty, another part was gripped by the story and wanted to return to the dreamscape to find out what happened.

As a kid I felt like an outsider—clumsy and inept, a loser at dodgeball—and I judged myself to be without much talent. That my dreaming produced vivid, colorful images and exciting dramas gave me hope. I valued each dream as a creative accomplishment and felt that even if my awake self was dull and unimaginative, my night self was a brave girl who faced wild animals and flew through the sky, a clever girl who escaped nasty situations and invented things no one had thought of yet. So I clung to her, my night self, for a sense of worth. And somehow, even when others let me down, no matter what, my dreams stuck with me. They spoke to me, kept me company, entertained me, scared me without hurting me, and were an endless source of marvel. My dreams introduced me to interesting characters, found long-forgotten friends, and, later in life, brought back loved ones who had passed on.

My interest in dreams led me to study psychology and, after several years of training, become a psychotherapist. In my work I found that, just as they did for me, dreams guided my clients—they were like an inner therapist. At times, when I didn't know what was best for a client, I turned to the inner source of wisdom communicated by the dream. I call that source the "dream maker." I could always count on a client's dream maker to point us in the right direction.

After I became a therapist and trained as a Jungian psychoanalyst, I taught and supervised at the Child Study Center, part of the Yale School of Medicine. There, therapists brought me the dreams of the children they worked with, many of whom had experienced unimaginable tragedy in their real lives. Somehow, the valiance of the human spirit prevailed in the children's dreams. Even under dire circumstances, a child might have rested their head at night amid unspeakable tumult and escaped the difficult reality of life to dream images of a sanctuary that kept all the frightening people and things away. Maybe you can relate to this—a difficult time in your life when your dreams helped you.

Having been sustained by dreams and having witnessed how helpful dreams were to others, I want to share my knowledge and experience to help you learn how to keep a dream journal, work with your dreams, and tap into this incredible resource within.

A dream journal is a special kind of journal. Unlike a personal journal or diary, a dream journal is structured to keep track of the date, the dream, and the life circumstances around the time of the dream. Connecting your daytime life with your dream life and keeping an ongoing record of your dreams will help you discover your personal dream language. You'll notice personal themes and see how helpful dreams can be in moving your life forward.

As you begin working on your dreams, what matters most is remembering, then journaling, the dream. Dreams can do so much for you. A dream can solve a problem you're struggling with, or even help you invent something the whole world needs. You have inner riches you haven't tapped into yet—creative impulses, insight, wisdom, and untouched feelings—and that's exciting.

Because your dreams are always moving you toward the fullest and best version of yourself, a dream may bring something to your attention you haven't yet noticed. By raising your awareness, you may be able to discover and name a problem—the first step in healing. This can be one of the greatest gifts dreams offer because every healing process begins with awareness. The dream maker only brings you memories, experiences, or situations you are ready to engage with. In a gentle way, this is your psyche's version of nudging you forward in life, past current obstacles and old hurts.

You may remember forgotten events or get a peek at the future. While working with your dreams, you may discover important issues that have been waiting for your attention. Sometimes this means an upsetting memory or past trauma that has been tucked away comes alive for you and brings with it intense emotions. If you come upon a serious issue you weren't aware of, don't ever feel ashamed about reaching out to a professional therapist for help. Journaling and interpreting your dreams is not a substitute for professional care.

One other point I'd like to make at the outset—every person has their own dream rhythm. Some folks remember five dreams every night. Some folks remember one dream each month; some catch a dream or two each year. Don't fret about quantity. You'll find your rhythm and it will be perfectly suited to you. Stay connected to your experience and don't be distracted by anyone else's pattern. Your curiosity and desire to learn will surely be rewarded. Your own dream life, no matter what shape it takes, is special, rich, unique, and meaningful. So, here we go.

DREAMS

Dreams are the images, emotions, experiences, characters, and sounds or conversations that occur during the night as we sleep. Dream language is primarily a language of images versus a language of words, and working with dreams is a little like learning a foreign language. In fact, dreams often communicate in metaphors by showing only an image. For example, imagine this dream: I am driving but, instead of a car, it's a lemon.

Throughout this book, I'll help you get the hang of understanding your dreams. You will learn how to record your dreams and how to pick out the main features of a dream. I'll offer prompts to help you develop dream work skills. You will practice translating images into meanings that will help you live your life better and more fully. The wise dream maker within you is always guiding you toward living your richest, most authentic, and magnificent life.

WHY WE DREAM

Most of us spend approximately one-third of our lives asleep. Of that sleep time, about half is spent in a state known as REM, an acronym for rapid eye movement. During this state we are, essentially, paralyzed and unable to move, but our closed eyes dance around rapidly and randomly. It is mostly during this phase of sleep, which usually begins about an hour and a half after we've fallen asleep, that we dream. During the night we usually cycle through REM states four or five times; each progressive cycle lasts a little longer, with the longest REM cycle occurring closest to when we wake.

Some folks say they don't dream; the truth is, they don't remember their dreams. Later, we'll go over some hints for helping you remember your dreams. We know from the discoveries of neuroscience that, even if dreams aren't remembered, dreaming is something all humans do.

Exactly why we dream remains somewhat of a mystery, but when it comes to the way the human body and its processes are so magnificently engineered for regulation, healing, and self-care, there are no mistakes. It would make no sense that dreaming serves no function. Dream researchers have found that dreams serve many functions. They help process the "residue" of the day. They prepare you for challenging future events. They consolidate memories and stash them in the right place in your brain. They inspire creativity. They sometimes communicate about diseases before they are diagnosed by a doctor. Dreams can even predict future events. Dreams are always on your side, always rooting for your success, pointing you in the direction of living your truest life, leading you away from harmful situations, and trying to prepare you for what's coming. They help you develop areas in which you might need strengthening. Your dreams are your best friend—an amazing resource just waiting to be tapped.

A VERY BRIEF HISTORY OF DREAM INTERPRETATION

Who knows the actual history of dream interpretation? For sure, long before human beings began writing, they were dreaming and talking about their dreams. In many indigenous cultures, even today, dreams are considered messages from the gods and are shared orally to benefit the entire community, not just the individual. In this way, the dreamer is considered the vehicle through which the divine message is transmitted.

The earliest recorded dream was written down in the third millennium BCE during the Mesopotamian civilization. Dumuzi, thought to be a ruler, dreamed a series of complicated events, often encapsulated as the image of an eagle swooping down, seizing a lamb from a flock of sheep. In the ancient literature, Dumuzi's sister, Geshtinanna, interpreted the dream for him and warned him of perilous events to come.

In biblical times, 21 dreams were recorded in text. In ancient Greece, dreams were held in great esteem. Asclepius, the god of medicine and son of Apollo, founded temples called Asclepieions. When sick, a person went to the temple, where they were escorted into its central chamber. There, the sick person was instructed to sleep, perhaps many nights, until a dream finally came. The dream was shared with the resident priest, who then prescribed the cure based on the dream's message.

All civilizations have paid attention to dreams. Some have recorded and interpreted the dreams in writing; others have handed down dream wisdom by oral tradition from generation to generation.

In modern times, Sigmund Freud published the first treatise on dreams, *The Interpretation of Dreams*, in 1900 in Vienna, Austria. At the time, Carl Jung was a young doctor working at a famous psychiatric hospital, the Burghölzli, in Zurich, Switzerland. Jung read Freud's book with tremendous enthusiasm and was so excited by Freud's ideas that he wrote to Freud and visited him in Vienna, thus beginning a fruitful relationship.

These two early founders of psychoanalytic thought collaborated intensely for a dozen years, and our modern approach to dream analysis began with them. Both geniuses in their own rights, Freud and Jung eventually parted ways. Among the disagreements they had was the nature of the unconscious and, particularly, the role of dreams. Freud felt the unconscious was a receptacle for forbidden or unwanted thoughts, primarily sexual ones, and that dreams represented unfulfilled wishes masquerading in other more benign forms. Jung, on the other hand, felt that, although dreams sometimes contained repressed thoughts or feelings and unfulfilled wishes, the unconscious and dreams held much greater value. Jung felt that dreams and the unconscious were the source of creativity and infinite inspiration and, across cultures, dreams contained universal themes he called archetypes.

At present, research into dream phenomena continues. Advances in technology, particularly the EEG, fMRI, and PET scan, enable researchers to study brain activity as it is happening, allowing neuroscientists to use this information to unlock the secrets of brain activity during sleep and dreaming. Anyone who has ever been moved, inspired, taught, or spiritually awakened by a dream will testify to the tremendous power, value, and transformative potential of dreams.

TYPES OF DREAMS

Dreams take many forms: nightmares, recurrent dreams, anxiety dreams, and lucid dreams, just to name a few. Sometimes you remember a little snippet of a dream and, other times, an intense dream will stay with you forever. Some dreams are so wonderful you don't want them to end; for others, you breathe a sigh of relief when you wake, thinking, *Thank goodness that was a dream.*

In addition to the different types, dreams have different shapes, patterns, or genres. A dream may be an adventure, a chase, a challenge, a discovery, an embarrassment, a journey, a romance, a visit, a reunion, a conflict, etc. Pay attention to this overall pattern regardless of whether it's sweet or terrifying. Knowing the storyline, or plot structure, of the dream can help you figure out its deeper meaning.

Recurring Dreams

A recurring dream is like a gentle tap on the shoulder, the dream maker saying, "Ahem, you didn't get the message." The same issue is still important—either you haven't dealt with it, or it hasn't been resolved. When you have repeating dreams, it's important to pay attention to them.

Recurring dreams will not always be exact replicas of one another. For example, I dreamed I had wax in my ear. Another version of this: A mouse chewed the wiring of the car radio. Another version: The doctor said I would have to get chemotherapy through the ear. Even though the dreams depict different imagery, the theme of hearing makes these dreams a repeating series. Each version of the dream is a little stronger and more insistent. Finally, after the third dream, the message got through—I needed to listen to some guidance I had been ignoring.

Nightmares

A nightmare is a frightening dream: in fact, one so scary it wakes you up. Survivors of traumatic events often suffer from nightmares relating to the trauma. The nightmare is a way the mind attempts to process the trauma, stress, and other emotionally overwhelming experiences. It is a normal way of coping; however, if a trauma-related nightmare continues over a long period, it may be a symptom of post-traumatic stress disorder and the dreamer should seek professional help.

Benign factors can also cause nightmares—eating late-night snacks, especially sugary ones, taking certain medications, or even sleeping at high altitude.

Nightmares can also occur at important transition points in life—graduation, a first job, marriage, childbirth, etc. In a peculiar way, a nightmare can be good news, not to the frightened dreamer, but to the future self. In the nightmare, the self represented in the dream is facing an overwhelming situation the dreamer feels unable to master and, therefore, finds terrifying. In this way, the nightmare can announce a period of coming growth but the future self (who will be able to face this situation) hasn't grown yet. The self in the dream is less developed than the person they will soon become.

Lucid Dreams

Lucid dreaming is the state of being aware you are dreaming *while* you are actually dreaming. You are both in the dream and aware you are having it. Centuries ago, Aristotle wrote about having an awareness of dreaming. In more recent times, the phenomenon of lucid dreaming has been studied, yet remains a mystery. Many lucid dreamers are not only aware of the dream but are also able to go back into the dream and shape events so they can influence the outcome of the dream.

Precognitive/Psychic/Prophetic Dreams

A dream can present a situation or an event that will happen in the future. I lived and worked in New York City at the time of the terrorist attack on the World Trade Center. I learned through the therapist grapevine that many people had precognitive dreams about this event. That information prompted me to conduct a daylong workshop titled "Dreams of 9/11." The auditorium was filled with dreamers who had premonitions of what was to happen. Several individuals dreamed specifically of planes crashing into skyscrapers. One woman dreamed that two ravens flew into the towers of the World Trade Center and caused them to crumble.

We don't know how information is transmitted. It seems that the unconscious is more attuned to unspoken patterns and able to catch certain vibrations beyond the capacity of the conscious mind.

Dreams of Current Situations

While working on this book, the COVID-19 pandemic first broke out. Many dream experts began collecting dreams as they were happening. In addition to the medical, financial, and social devastation, this particular situation caused worldwide panic and fear. Besides themes relating specifically to the virus, such as an unseen enemy, one of the most ubiquitous themes that began to appear in dreams worldwide was that loved ones who had passed on, particularly mothers and fathers, showed up in very sweet, nurturing ways. It would seem that when so many folks were feeling very scared, dream images of parents were of comfort, offering advice, warmth, and love. Images specifically associated with the pandemic will carry new universal and symbolic meaning moving forward. And future collective events will inevitably generate new meanings and associations for the images associated with those events.

Daydreams

Daydreaming is a state somewhere between being awake and being asleep. Our usual level of consciousness drops, making room for something from the unconscious to emerge. Another aspect of daydreaming is a throwaway thought. Out of the blue, something comes to mind. Usually you say to yourself, "Oh, that's ridiculous," and you dismiss the thought. Both daydreams and throwaway thoughts are worth noting for the information they hold.

Sometimes these thoughts inform us about our desires or unconscious worries. One of the best things about daydreams is their ability to help us escape from a current situation that is boring or otherwise unpleasant. In tuning out of the situation, we tune in to ourselves.

Other dreamlike phenomena, hypnagogic (falling asleep) and hypnopompic (waking up) hallucinations, occur just on the brink of sleep and waking. In them, a person has a dreamlike experience that feels very real. These can be disturbing and, if they recur, may suggest conditions that should be drawn to the attention of a physician.

Big Dreams and Little Dreams

Indigenous shamans distinguish between big and little dreams. Little dreams are the ordinary ones that help you process the residue of the day, secure memory, and maintain sleep. Most often, these dreams evaporate quickly unless you make a special effort to anchor them, either by writing them down or sharing them with another person.

Big dreams, on the other hand, make an indelible impression, often staying with you for a long time, or even your whole life. These are dreams usually of epic proportion, with intense emotional tones and vivid imagery. Rather than processing the recent aspects of your life, these dreams often announce big changes coming or that have occurred.

WHY YOU SHOULD KEEP A DREAM JOURNAL

The most important reason for keeping a dream journal is that you have an inner sage trying to communicate their wisdom to you. The dreaming self has a different perspective than the awake self. It knows you, sometimes better than you know yourself.

I remember a dream I had shortly after I moved in with a boyfriend. I was crazy about this man. A handsome fellow, he had an outstanding career, was extraordinarily wealthy, and was in love with me. I thought I had grabbed the brass ring on the merry-go-round. The dream I had the night I moved into his apartment was of an old woman telling me I had moved into a slum. Guess what?

It took a while for me to learn but, eventually, I discovered that, in spite of the affluence, living with him also included emotional impoverishment.

Sometimes the dream will give you guidance that you don't want at the moment, like the scenario I just mentioned. By writing down the dream, at a later date you may be able to grasp what the dream maker saw. Also, sometimes a dream takes a long time to reveal its meaning. Your journal enables you to go back and understand situations better, and often gain deeper and deeper insight into the challenges you faced.

In your dream life, of course, you will have experiences you don't have in your waking life. For example, you might dream you are bitten by a snake. When you wake, there are no fang marks on your body, yet you have had an experience that expands your awareness. Because of your dream, you will have knowledge of, and empathy for, experiences you have never lived in your waking life. In this way, many inventors, authors, musicians, and artists credit their dreams as the origin of their creative endeavors.

By keeping a dream journal, you will discover themes and patterns specific to you. Certain images will occur frequently because they are personal symbols. As you learn your personal patterns, symbols, and imagery, your appreciation of your unique individuality will expand. You will know yourself better. And who knows? You may even join the ranks of those whose inventions emerge from their dreams.

Record Your Experience

Recording your dream experience is simple but important. When you wake in the morning, record your dream by writing down the date, the dream, and the significant or out-of-the-ordinary experiences of the day or days preceding the dream. The best way to do this is to keep your dream journal beside your bed, along with a pen or pencil. When you wake, do not immediately jump out of bed. Lie still with your eyes closed for a few minutes to try to catch the dream. Sometimes you will wake in the middle of the night, aware you've had a dream. Try to scribble down a few words to help you remember the main part, but don't turn on the light or try to capture the whole thing. Although remembering a dream and keeping your journal matter, don't let the process interfere with getting a good night's sleep.

Some people are very resistant to writing down dreams. If that is the case for you, try speaking your dream into your phone's recording app. You could also tell your partner or a close friend about the dream. The most important thing about remembering or recording a dream is that most dreams naturally "evaporate." You think you'll remember it, but you won't. It will be gone before you finish your first cup of coffee. Even if you think that what you remember is small or unimportant, it's worth recording.

As I mentioned earlier, I remembered dreams when I was a child; however, I only began writing them down as a young adult. Now, when I look back over those dreams, I love having the experience of remembering the dreams all over again, especially noting the details of the "big dreams." Having the record of my dreams, I look back on my younger self with gentler eyes and much more love and appreciation than I had at the time. I wish that for you, too.

Track Common Elements, Symbols, and Signs

You have your personal mythology. Certain images, places, and experiences mean more to you than they mean to others. This is part of your individuality and uniqueness. Your dreams will help you recognize and appreciate the importance of these elements. Here's something wonderful about dreams: They present us with images that aren't influenced by what others think is cool or what advertising tells us we should like. The dream stands apart from these external pressures and presents us with images, symbols, and elements that are authentic, from a deep, interior place.

Make Note of Your Insights, Reflections, and Breakthroughs

I hope you will come back to these pages often. As you keep track of your dreams over time, you'll notice patterns, recurrent themes, and familiar relationship conflicts or pleasures. You'll understand certain issues that reappear. You will notice that figures evolve and show signs of growth. You will notice many trends in your dream life. Take the time to gather the data, consider it, and draw some tentative insights. If your dream has delivered any surprising picture of a current situation, make a note of that with the date. Just as I shared with you the dream I had when I moved into my boyfriend's apartment, it took me a year to realize what the unconscious noticed immediately. Recognizing and recording the dream maker's insights into your life's situations help you recognize, respect, and trust your inner wisdom. If you keep track of your dreams, you will discover you are smarter and more aware than you think.

HOW TO USE THIS JOURNAL

As you approach learning about your dreams, you'll need to figure out what works best for you. Your journey into your dream life is not like anyone else's and it needs to be tailored to your lifestyle, your time constraints, your sleeping patterns, and your dream rhythm.

Begin by recording your dreams and responding to the guided prompts in part 1. You may not completely understand some suggestions, but an exercise like this awakens the imaginative image-making part of your brain. It can be fun and, if you enjoy it, don't limit yourself to doing the prompt just once. Grab some blank pieces of paper and do it many times. The more you work with the material, the better you will become at navigating the meaning of your dreams. In part 2, I'll walk you through how to interpret your dreams and explore some of the most common signs, symbols, and meanings.

The habit of journaling will be a most rewarding long-term experience. One day, you'll remember that, a year ago, you dreamed of something that rings a bell with the dream you had last night. Being able to go back and access that dream is so satisfying, and it will likely bring you fresh and deeper insights.

The basic form I suggest for recording your dream is to date it, write down the significant events of the preceding day or so, and record the content of the dream as you remember it. Write down as much detail as you can. If you have long, complicated dreams or are a prolific dreamer, do not make this process so onerous that writing the dream takes too much time or becomes a dreaded chore. Write shorthand or just list key elements of the dream.

For example, that dream I had about moving in with my boyfriend could have gone something like this:

2/10/12

Moved into JB's apt.

Giddy and happy

Old woman, "Slum."

I call this "anchoring" the dream. The anchoring process is most effective when you do it by writing. Only the most vivid or terrifying dreams become indelibly etched in your memory. So, click your pen or sharpen your pencil.

You're ready to go!

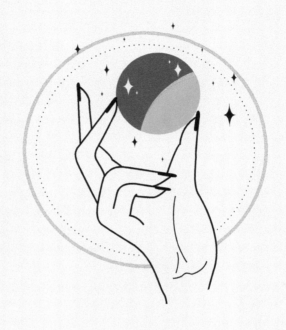

MAN IS A GENIUS
WHEN HE IS DREAMING.

—AKIRA KUROSAWA

Part I

Explore your Dreams

This section of your dream journal is all about getting into the habit of recording your dreams and working with them. The pages ahead include lines for dating and recording your dreams. The facing pages include prompts and space to respond. The prompts are short exercises designed to help you dig in and discover the meaning within the dream.

The more you work with your dreams, the more insight they yield. Your journal is designed so all the guidance and exercises in the prompts point you toward a deeper connection with, and understanding of, your dream life. The skills you will develop when you complete the prompts will enable you to become more proficient in utilizing the wisdom contained in the dreams.

At first you may dismiss a dream as being unimportant. Often, you'll think, *This makes no sense.* Or maybe, *I don't want to know what this means.* Or, *I did something so embarrassing in this dream, I am not going to write it for fear someone might read it.* I encourage you not to judge your dream self by the standards of your awake self. If you find your dream self tearing down the street naked or showing up at work topless—don't worry. It probably means something like you are feeling overexposed, or you need to be more exposed, or you're afraid something you prefer to keep private might be revealed.

This brings me to another principle of dream interpretation. You may read in another book or hear from another dream coach that every character of the dream represents a part of you. I don't subscribe to this principle completely. You can try it on with certain figures to see how it lands for you. My view is that, sometimes, scary or evil figures appear in your dream; I never want you to fear that this monster lurks inside you. The terrible figure may be symbolically related to an opposite counterpart in your waking life. For example, an overly cautious person may find a reckless person in their dream. When a frightening figure appears, it is also entirely possible there is someone or something in your life space that is much more dangerous, threatening, or even evil, than you are consciously aware of.

The following prompts are meant to build your dream work skills, to be inspiring, and, above all, fun. Naturally, certain prompts will land differently than others. You may sail through some; others may feel like they need a bit of mental or emotional elbow grease to complete. If you find prompts that open you up and there isn't enough space for everything you want to write—you've hit pay dirt. Grab a loose piece of paper or another journal and keep writing; come back to this prompt with another dream. This is your journal and it's important to determine which approaches work best for you.

The key to these prompts and recording your dreams is to enjoy the process. Be curious. Your dream is an outside-the-box creation— approach it that way. One of the therapeutic methods always part of dream work is "free association." This means letting your imagination or memory take you wherever it wants to go, without resistance, inhibition, or restriction. Let your dream work take you to a boundless space where you are free just to be yourself.

WAYS TO DREAM BETTER

The <u>most</u> important thing you can do to dream better is to sleep better. Here are some recommendations for sleeping, and consequently, dreaming better:

- **Eliminate electronics.** I know this is tough, but remove ALL electronic equipment from the bedroom. I mean ALL, including e-readers, smartphones, screens, the works. Read from a paper book before going to sleep. Choose something soothing, maybe even a little boring.

- **Avoid clutter.** Keep a tidy, uncluttered bedroom.

- **Reduce the temperature at night.** A cool, dark, quiet room is most conducive to good sleep.

- **Be prepared.** Place this journal or a notebook and pen on the nightstand beside your bed to make it easy for you to scribble a few notes to "catch" your dream.

- **Find your rhythm.** Do you know what your natural sleep rhythm is? To find it, you'll need to give yourself a couple weeks to go to sleep and rise without a schedule. Sleeping according to your inner clock is so much better for you than sleeping according to an alarm clock.

- **Set an intention.** Before you go to sleep, set an intention by asking for a dream. Another way to set an intention is to write a note to your dream maker asking for a dream focused on a particular issue. For example: Dear Dream Maker, My boss and I don't seem to be on the same wavelength. Can you send me a dream that helps me figure out my end of things?

- **Meditate.** Do a short meditation. Imagine something especially comforting. Let that image come as alive as possible as you breathe deeply and slowly.

- **Visualize a dream.** If you've recently had a dream, after you turn off the light, bring that dream to mind. Try to enter it as fully as you can, looking around the dreamscape to notice the details you might not have noticed before. It doesn't have to be exactly what you remember. Making up details can work well.

- **Wake mindfully.** Upon waking, lie still with your eyes closed for a few minutes and try to "catch" a thread of a dream. One image, one color, one person—any small detail can be the portal to more. Write down whatever you can remember in your journal. It often happens that by writing down one detail, later in the day something you see or hear will trigger a memory of the dream—and the whole thing comes tumbling back.

- **Change things up.** Climb into bed from the other side. Disrupting familiar and habitual patterns is like cracking open the window between the unconscious and conscious mind—fresh air always blows in.

- **Change up your energy.** In my experience, any location where nature is especially predominant amps up my dream life—a mountain top, the beach, a deep forest. Take a trip to a place that gives you energy.

Although these tips will help you sleep and dream better, you may not be able to follow them all—that's okay. Each tip you follow will increase your likelihood of long, quality sleep and the dreams you seek.

TIPS FOR REMEMBERING DREAMS

You don't need any tips for remembering "big dreams." The dreams that need anchoring are the smaller dreams, ones that routinely occur every night. Here are a few more tips that will help you remember your dreams:

- **Wake up early.** If you are having trouble remembering any dreams at all, set an alarm clock for one hour before your usual wake-up time. Don't set an alarm that goes off like a fire alarm and throws you out of bed. When you wake up at this unfamiliar time, lie quietly with your eyes closed to see whether you can catch any part of a dream.

- **Name it.** If you are able to catch your dream when you wake, give it a title.

- **Illustrate an image.** Choose one image from your dream and, instead of writing down the dream, draw the object in your dream journal.

- **Spark your memory.** After recording your dream in your journal, write a few key words on a sticky note or small piece of paper. Tuck it into your pocket. During the day, take it out, read what you have written, and see if you can bring the memory of the dream back. Doing this will help you stay connected to your dream and is likely to invite another dream.

- **Note key images.** Over time, as you write down your dreams, consider keeping a list of images that recur. You have your unique language of images—things that speak to you most deeply. Paying special attention to yours will make it easier to remember them when they occur.

DATE: 10/11

Record Your Dream Here

I was with my family
and Jimmy/Nick was with
his new girlfriend and I
was sending off to Italy
and everyone was nice to him
but he ignored me/mean to me.
His girlfriend didn't even understand
the trama. At the end I got him
to talk to me and he was
mean & we let the cats out?

Where did your dream take place? What are your significant memories about this place? Why would your dream take you there?

A house I have never been there was a tent we broke down large porch. A place for closure? Wood porch. Family room? Reminded me of nini tdas old place

Write down three things you are most excited about as you learn to work with your dreams. What are your hopes as you begin this endeavor?

To understand meaning behind my subconcious.
Hopes to learn

DATE: _____

Record Your Dream Here

_____

_____

_____

_____

_____

_____

_____

_____

_____

_____

_____

_____

_____

_____

Identify the most important element of your dream. It could be a person, place, object, interaction, or emotion. What is the most important thing about this element? Why would your dream bring this to you?

_____

_____

_____

_____

_____

Is there something you are afraid your dreams will reveal? If so, write down that fear. You don't have to write down exactly what you fear might be revealed; instead, write a bit about your fear and how you might be affected by it.

_____

_____

_____

_____

_____

_____

DATE: _____

Record Your Dream Here

_____

_____

_____

_____

_____

_____

_____

_____

_____

_____

_____

_____

_____

_____

_____

_____

_____

_____

_____

Give your dream a title.

_____

_____

_____

_____

_____

With whom would you most like to share this dream? Write a few lines about why this person would be a good choice.

_____

_____

_____

_____

_____

_____

_____

_____

DATE: _____

Record Your Dream Here

_____

_____

_____

_____

_____

_____

_____

_____

_____

_____

_____

_____

_____

Who showed up in your dream last night? What is that person's significance? Why would that person make a dream visit?

_____

_____

_____

_____

_____

Have you ever dreamed of a famous person? If so, who? What is that person's role in larger society? Why would that person make a dream visit? Does their presence offer any clues about what you might discover about yourself?

_____

_____

_____

_____

_____

DATE: _____

Record Your Dream Here

_____

_____

_____

_____

_____

_____

_____

_____

_____

_____

_____

_____

_____

_____

_____

_____

What was the emotion of your dream last night? What color would you give that emotion? Why would your dream maker want you to experience that emotion?

Have you ever had a nightmare? If so, write about it.

DATE: _____

Record Your Dream Here

What's the best thing about the dream you just had?

When you imagine your future, what is the best dream you can imagine having?

DATE: _____

Record Your Dream Here

_____

_____

_____

_____

_____

_____

_____

_____

_____

_____

_____

_____

_____

_____

_____

_____

Choose one detail from your dream. Why would that particular detail show up in the dream? Can you think of it as a symbol? If so, write down what it might represent or mean to you.

_____

_____

_____

_____

_____

What changes are you thinking about making in your life? Is there an image you have dreamed of recently that might give you a clue about how to make that change?

_____

_____

_____

_____

_____

DATE: _____

Record Your Dream Here

_____

_____

_____

_____

_____

_____

_____

_____

_____

_____

_____

_____

_____

_____

What is the genre of the dream you had last night? Was it an adventure? A conflict? A challenge? A romance? An embarrassment? Something else? Write a description of the theme or pattern the dream expressed.

What situations do you dream about regularly? Why might your dreams present these scenarios?

DATE: _____

Record Your Dream Here

_____

_____

_____

_____

_____

_____

_____

_____

_____

_____

_____

_____

_____

_____

_____

_____

After writing down your dream, close your eyes for a minute and imagine you are able to go back into the dream. Write down what it feels like. Also, write down any details you notice when you go back into your dream.

_____

_____

_____

_____

_____

What did your dream self do last night? Was it something your awake self would do? If there is a difference, what can this tell you about yourself?

_____

_____

_____

_____

_____

DATE: _____

Record Your Dream Here

_____

_____

_____

_____

_____

_____

_____

_____

_____

_____

_____

_____

_____

_____

Pick an object from your dream. Imagine explaining it to someone who has never heard of such a thing. Can you describe the object in enough detail to convey its function here on Earth? How is it meaningful to you?

What was the emotion of your dream last night? Can you name another time, or times, when you felt that emotion? Write about those times.

DATE: _____

Record Your Dream Here

_____

_____

_____

_____

_____

_____

_____

_____

_____

_____

_____

_____

Choose one detail from your dream. Why would that particular detail show up in the dream? Can you think of it as a symbol? If so, write down what it might represent or mean to you.

_____

_____

_____

_____

_____

_____

Write a message to your dream maker asking for help with a current problem in your daily life. It doesn't matter if it's a big problem or a small one.

_____

_____

_____

_____

_____

_____

DATE:

Record Your Dream Here

After writing down your dream, describe how the dream ended. For example, was a conflict resolved? Was a secret uncovered? Were things left unfinished? What could the ending tell you about what's going on in your life now?

What's the best thing about the dream you just had?

DATE: _____

Record Your Dream Here

_____

_____

_____

_____

_____

_____

_____

_____

_____

_____

_____

_____

_____

_____

_____

Who showed up in your dream last night? What is that person's significance? Why would that person make a dream visit?

_____

_____

_____

_____

_____

What did your dream self do last night? Was it something your awake self would do? If there is a difference, what can this tell you about yourself?

_____

_____

_____

_____

_____

DATE: _____

Record Your Dream Here

Underline the most important element of your dream. It could be a person, place, object, interaction, or emotion. What is the significance of this element? Why might your dream bring this to you?

_____

_____

_____

_____

_____

Write a message of gratitude to your dream maker for sending you an especially meaningful dream image. The image does not have to be from your most recent dream.

_____

_____

_____

_____

_____

DATE: _____

Record Your Dream Here

_____

_____

_____

_____

_____

_____

_____

_____

_____

_____

_____

_____

_____

_____

_____

_____

If you've had a long, complicated dream where so many images call for your attention, it's hard to know where to start. After you record the dream, create a sentence or two that summarizes or condenses the dream. Summarizing an epic dream is often a good place to begin understanding it.

With whom would you most like to share a dream? Write a few lines about why this person would be a good choice.

DATE: _____

Record Your Dream Here

What was the emotion of your dream last night? What color would you give that emotion? Why would your dream want you to experience that emotion?

_____

_____

_____

_____

_____

Nightmares give us an experience we're usually not eager to repeat. If you can recall a nightmare, can you think of one reason this nightmare was a good preparatory experience for something else?

_____

_____

_____

_____

_____

DATE:

Record Your Dream Here

Choose one detail from your dream. Why would that particular detail show up in the dream? Can you think of it as a symbol? If so, write down what it might represent or mean to you.

What situations do you dream about regularly? Why might your dreams present these scenarios?

DATE: _____

Record Your Dream Here

_____

_____

_____

_____

_____

_____

_____

_____

_____

_____

_____

_____

_____

What old behaviors or obstacles are you working to overcome? Can you find any messages related to this growth in your recent dreams? If so, write about what you glean. If not, write down what you would like help with.

What is the most outrageous thing you can remember ever having done in a dream? Write that down here.

DATE: _____

Record Your Dream Here

_____

_____

_____

_____

_____

_____

_____

_____

_____

_____

_____

_____

_____

_____

_____

Choose one object in your dream. Create an imaginary conversation with that object, even if it is not a person.

Is there anything you would like added to your life? Imagine a dream that would foretell bringing that to you.

DATE: _____

Record Your Dream Here

_____

_____

_____

_____

_____

_____

_____

_____

_____

_____

_____

_____

_____

_____

Identify the most important element of your dream. It could be a person, place, object, interaction, or emotion. What is the most important thing about this element? Why would your dream bring this to you?

_____

_____

_____

_____

_____

_____

What changes are you thinking about making in your life? Is there an image you have dreamed of recently that might be offering a clue about how to make that change?

_____

_____

_____

_____

_____

_____

DATE:

Record Your Dream Here

Who showed up in your dream last night? What is that person's significance? Why would that person make a dream visit?

_____

_____

_____

_____

_____

Other than you, which people show up most often in your dreams? Make a list of those people and their relationships to you.

_____

_____

_____

_____

_____

DATE: _____

Record Your Dream Here

_____

_____

_____

_____

_____

_____

_____

_____

_____

_____

_____

_____

_____

_____

_____

Where did your dream take place? What are your significant memories about this place? Why would your dream take place there?

_____

_____

_____

_____

_____

_____

What is the earliest dream you can remember? Write about it here.

_____

_____

_____

_____

_____

_____

_____

_____

DATE: _____

Record Your Dream Here

_____

_____

_____

_____

_____

_____

_____

_____

_____

_____

_____

_____

_____

_____

What is the genre of the dream you had last night? Was it an adventure? A conflict? A challenge? A romance? An embarrassment? Something else? After recording the dream, write a description of the theme or pattern the dream expressed.

Make up a dream you would like to come true. Describe the dream in detail and end it with your wish coming true.

DATE:

Record Your Dream Here

What was the emotion of your dream last night? What color would you give that emotion? Why would your dream want you to experience that emotion?

If you have nightmares or scary dreams, is there a particular theme that repeats? For example, some people often dream of flooding, or fires, or falling, etc. What could your unconscious be trying to tell you?

DATE: _____

Record Your Dream Here

_____

_____

_____

_____

_____

_____

_____

_____

_____

_____

_____

_____

_____

_____

_____

_____

_____

_____

Where did your dream take place? What are your significant memories about this place? Why would your dream take place there?

_____

_____

_____

_____

_____

If you have ever dreamed of your childhood home, what room did you dream about? What are the most significant events that occurred in that room? Write down what you remember about that room.

_____

_____

_____

_____

_____

DATE: _____

Record Your Dream Here

_____

_____

_____

_____

_____

_____

_____

_____

_____

_____

_____

_____

_____

Choose a dream you experience as disturbing, sad, or frightening. Write one new ending to the dream.

_____

_____

_____

_____

_____

_____

How frequently do you dream of work? What is the theme or emotion most often associated with this kind of dream?

_____

_____

_____

_____

_____

_____

_____

_____

DATE:

Record Your Dream Here

After writing down your dream, describe how the dream ended. For example, was a conflict resolved? Was a secret uncovered? Were things left unfinished? What could the ending tell you about what's going on in your life now?

_____

_____

_____

_____

_____

_____

If you can remember past dreams, write them here and try to approximate when you had them.

_____

_____

_____

_____

_____

_____

DATE: _____

Record Your Dream Here

_____

_____

_____

_____

_____

_____

_____

_____

_____

_____

_____

_____

_____

After writing down your dream, close your eyes for a minute and imagine you are able to go back into the dream. Write down what it feels like. Also, write down any details you notice when you go back into your dream.

_____

_____

_____

_____

_____

_____

Have you had a dream recently that included a strong emotion? If so, why would your dream maker want you to experience that?

_____

_____

_____

_____

_____

_____

DATE: _____

Record Your Dream Here

_____

_____

_____

_____

_____

_____

_____

_____

_____

_____

_____

_____

Review your dreams to determine whether there is a repeating pattern. For example, you might have a number of dreams about work, or they might be about family. Maybe you are chased often. Or maybe the same emotion recurs in different settings. Can you find a theme? Write it down. Does this offer insight into what your dreaming self is working on?

When you envision your future, what is the best dream you can imagine having?

DATE: _____

Record Your Dream Here

Identify the most important element of your dream. It could be a person, place, object, interaction, or emotion. What is the most important thing about this element? Why might your dream bring this to you?

_____

_____

_____

_____

Have you ever dreamed of a person, animal, or object that didn't exist? If so, describe that invention here. (Many scientists and creative individuals were inspired by images from their dreams. You might just be the next dream innovator!)

_____

_____

_____

_____

_____

DATE:

Record Your Dream Here

Where did your dream take place? What are your significant memories about this place? Why would your dream take place there?

Do your dreams take you back to certain places often? What places show up most frequently in your dreams? What do these places mean for you, symbolically?

DATE: _____

Record Your Dream Here

Sometimes dreams present situations that seem "off." For example, I am lounging around on a rubber float that belongs in a pool, but I'm in the ocean and there are sharks swimming all around. Situations like that are often attempts to call your attention to something in life that is out of kilter. Look back through your dreams and make a list of "out-of-kilter" situations. What can you learn from them?

What are the main themes of your dreams at this time? Write them down. After recording your dreams for a longer period, repeat the exercise to see whether the themes change or remain the same.

DATE: _____

Record Your Dream Here

What is the strangest thing your dream self has ever done?
Do you have any idea why they did that? What might that
part of the dream be expressing?

_____

_____

_____

_____

_____

Rather than writing down your dream, sketch it. Don't worry
about artistic ability. Use stick figures or any other shapes,
but try to capture the scene visually.

DATE:

Record Your Dream Here

What was the emotion of your dream last night? Can you think of another time you had this emotion? Was it stronger or weaker then? Write about this emotion.

_____

_____

_____

_____

_____

After you record a dream, look at it and think about changing one thing. What would that be? Write down that one thing, then explain why you would make that change.

_____

_____

_____

_____

_____

DATE: _____

Record Your Dream Here

_____

_____

_____

_____

_____

_____

_____

_____

_____

_____

_____

_____

_____

_____

_____

_____

_____

Choose one detail from your dream. Why would that particular detail show up in the dream? Can you think of it as a symbol? If so, write down what it might represent or mean to you.

Have you ever had a recurring dream? If so, what was the theme? What message could the dream be trying to convey?

DATE: _____

Record Your Dream Here

_____

_____

_____

_____

_____

_____

_____

_____

_____

_____

_____

_____

_____

_____

_____

Choose one object in your dream. Imagine that object has the ability to ask you three questions. Write down those questions.

_____

_____

_____

_____

Make an image map. To do this, choose one image from your dream and write it below. Draw a circle around it. Then, draw a larger circle around that circle and fill it with as many personal associations to the image you can think of. The purpose of this exercise is to open and deepen the understanding, connections, and personal meaning of the image.

DATE: _____

Record Your Dream Here

_____

_____

_____

_____

_____

_____

_____

_____

_____

_____

_____

_____

_____

_____

_____

Transformation is a common theme in dreams. An example might be that a man turns into a potato or a woman grows a beard. Go back through your dreams to see whether you find an image of transformation. What is that transformation? What might that mean symbolically?

Being unprepared is a common dream image. Have you ever had a dream of being unprepared? If so, what was the context? What anxiety did the dream represent for you?

DATE: _____

Record Your Dream Here

What was the most unexpected event in a recent dream?

_____

_____

_____

_____

_____

Write down the sparsest dream you can remember having.
Maybe it's just a color. Or an animal. Or a sound. Or a person.
Perhaps it was just one image. What can you take away from
the dream? Why might your dream maker send that image?

_____

_____

_____

_____

_____

_____

DATE: _____

Record Your Dream Here

_____

_____

_____

_____

_____

_____

_____

_____

_____

_____

_____

_____

_____

_____

Give your dream a title.

Choose an object from a dream—one that really speaks to you or captures your feelings. Write that word in the blank space below. Now, think of a word that comes to mind in association with your base word. Write it down and draw a line connecting the two words. Keep doing this, adding associated words and drawing lines between the word you think of and the word that triggered it. In the end, you should have many words all connected, kind of like a spider's web.

DATE: _____

Record Your Dream Here

Identify the most important element of your dream. It could be a person, place, object, interaction, or emotion. What is the most important thing about this element? Why might your dream bring this to you?

_____

_____

_____

_____

Is there an image or symbol from your dreams you are curious about? What ideas do you have about that image? Where does that image appear in the real world? Does it stand for any universal meaning? What does it mean to you?

_____

_____

_____

_____

_____

DATE:

Record Your Dream Here

Where did your dream take place? What are your significant memories about this place? Why would your dream take place there?

_____

_____

_____

_____

_____

Do certain animals, objects, people, or places show up in your dreams regularly? If so, write them down and then write a few lines about why you think they show up. (They may be the beginning of a personal system of symbols.)

_____

_____

_____

_____

_____

DATE: _____

Record Your Dream Here

_____

_____

_____

_____

_____

_____

_____

_____

_____

_____

_____

_____

_____

_____

What is the genre of the dream you had last night? Was it an adventure? A conflict? A challenge? A romance? An embarrassment? Something else? After recording the dream, write a description of the theme or pattern the dream expressed.

_____

_____

_____

_____

_____

Write a message to your dream maker asking for help with a current problem in your daily life.

_____

_____

_____

_____

_____

DATE: _____

Record Your Dream Here

After writing down your dream, describe how the dream ended. For example, was a conflict resolved? Was a secret uncovered? Were things left unfinished? What can the ending tell you about what's going on in your life now? Would you like to imagine a different ending? If so, write that down.

What's the best thing about the dream you just had?

DATE: _____

Record Your Dream Here

Choose one detail from your dream. Imagine the dream going in a completely different direction. Write down the new dream you are able to imagine from that detail.

_____

_____

_____

_____

_____

Close your eyes for a minute and imagine you are able to go back into the dream. Write down what it feels like. Also, write down any new details you notice when you go back into your dream.

_____

_____

_____

_____

_____

DATE: _____

Record Your Dream Here

What was the emotion of your dream last night? What would happen if you enlarged that emotion? What would happen if you shrank it? Write down what you notice about the range of emotion of your dream.

_____

_____

_____

_____

_____

_____

Write a message of gratitude to your dream maker for sending you an especially meaningful image.

_____

_____

_____

_____

_____

_____

DATE: _____

Record Your Dream Here

Who showed up in your dream last night? When was the last time you saw that person? What happened then? How might that be related to your dream? Why would that person make a dream visit?

_____

_____

_____

_____

_____

Have you had a dream recently that included a strong emotion? If so, why would your dream maker want you to experience that?

_____

_____

_____

_____

_____

DATE: _____

Record Your Dream Here

_____

_____

_____

_____

_____

_____

_____

_____

_____

_____

_____

_____

_____

_____

_____

What's the happiest thing about the dream you just had?
Even if that dream was a nightmare, was there anything to be
happy about in the dream? What was it?

After you record a dream, look at it and think about changing
one thing. What would that be? Write down that one thing,
then explain why you would make that change.

DATE: _____

Record Your Dream Here

_____

_____

_____

_____

_____

_____

_____

_____

_____

_____

_____

_____

_____

Identify the most important element of your dream. It could be a person, place, object, interaction, or emotion. What is the most important thing about this element? Why might your dream bring this to you?

_____

_____

_____

_____

_____

With whom would you most like to share this dream? Write a few lines about why this person would be a good choice.

_____

_____

_____

_____

_____

_____

DATE:

Record Your Dream Here

What is the genre of the dream you had last night? Was it an adventure? A conflict? A challenge? A romance? An embarrassment? Something else? After recording the dream, write a description of the theme or pattern the dream expressed.

_____

_____

_____

_____

_____

_____

Make up a dream you would like to come true. Describe the dream in detail and end it with your wish coming true.

_____

_____

_____

_____

_____

_____

DATE: _____

Record Your Dream Here

Choose one object in your dream. Imagine that object has the ability to give you guidance about a question on your mind. Write down the wisdom offered.

_____

_____

_____

_____

_____

Rather than writing down your dream, sketch it. Don't worry about artistic ability. Use stick figures or any other shapes, but try to capture the scene visually.

DATE: _____

Record Your Dream Here

_____

_____

_____

_____

_____

_____

_____

_____

_____

_____

_____

_____

_____

_____

Do your dreams take you back to certain places often? What places show up most frequently in your dreams? What do these places mean for you, symbolically?

Choose a color that represents "happy" to you. Get a marker in that color. Go back through your dreams and use the marker to circle anything that makes you feel happy. Make a list of those things here.

DATE: _____

Record Your Dream Here

What was the emotion of your dream last night? What color would you give that emotion? Why might your dream want you to experience that emotion?

_____

_____

_____

_____

_____

_____

Choose a color that represents "sad" to you. Get a marker in that color. Go back through your dreams and use the marker to circle anything that makes you sad. Make a list of those things here.

_____

_____

_____

_____

_____

DATE: _____

Record Your Dream Here

_____

_____

_____

_____

_____

_____

_____

_____

_____

_____

_____

_____

_____

_____

_____

_____

What is the genre of the dream you had last night? Was it an adventure? A conflict? A challenge? A romance? An embarrassment? Something else? After recording the dream, write a description of the theme or pattern the dream expressed.

What's the best thing about the dream you just had?

DATE: _____

Record Your Dream Here

_____

_____

_____

_____

_____

_____

_____

_____

_____

_____

_____

Choose one detail from your dream. Why would that particular detail show up in the dream? Can you think of it as a symbol? If so, write down what it might represent or mean to you.

_____

_____

_____

_____

_____

Write a message to your dream maker asking for help with a current problem in your daily life.

_____

_____

_____

_____

_____

DATE:

Record Your Dream Here

Who showed up in your dream last night? Imagine expanding the conversation with that person. What would you like them to know? Why would that person make a dream visit?

_____

_____

_____

_____

_____

_____

With whom would you most like to share a recent dream? Write about why this person would be a good choice.

_____

_____

_____

_____

_____

_____

DATE:

Record Your Dream Here

After writing down your dream, close your eyes for a minute and imagine you are able to go back into the dream. Write down what it feels like. Also, write down any details you notice when you go back into your dream.

Where did your dream take place? What are your significant memories about this place? Why would your dream take place there?

DATE: _____

Record Your Dream Here

Choose one object in your dream. Imagine that object has the ability to ask you three questions. Write down those questions.

_____

_____

_____

_____

_____

Write a message to your dream maker asking for information about them. Ask the dream maker what's coming up for you.

_____

_____

_____

_____

_____

_____

DATE:

Record Your Dream Here

Choose a color that represents "scary" to you. Get a marker in that color. Go back through your journal and use the marker to highlight anything that makes you feel scared. Make a list of those things here.

What did your dream self do last night? Was it something your awake self would do? If there is a difference, what can this tell you about yourself?

DATE: _____

Record Your Dream Here

_____

_____

_____

_____

_____

_____

_____

_____

_____

_____

_____

_____

_____

_____

_____

_____

Do certain animals, objects, people, or places show up in your dreams regularly? If so, write them down and then write a few lines about why you think they show up. (They may be the beginning of a personal system of symbols.)

What are the main themes of your dreams at this time? Write them down. After you have been recording your dreams for a longer period, repeat the exercise to see whether the themes change or remain the same.

DATE: _____

Record Your Dream Here

Identify the most important element of your dream. It could be a person, place, object, interaction, or emotion. What is the most important thing about this element? Why might your dream bring this to you?

Look back over your dreams and examine how you have color-coded them. Without looking at the content of the dreams, and only looking at the colors, what can you discover about your dreaming self?

A dream that is not interpreted
is like a letter that is not read.
—Talmud

Part II

INTerpreT your Dreams

When interpreting your dreams, get ready for some fun. Stow your guilt, embarrassment, and self-consciousness in a little box, lock it up, and tuck it away under the bed, or maybe in the attic. Attitudes of judgment will hinder your curiosity and openness, which are the things you need to expand your thinking.

The language of dreams is different from our spoken language. Understanding dream language isn't like learning Spanish or French, where specific words have specific meanings. The images of dreams are symbols—they aren't signs. A sign usually has a specific and fixed correspondence, like a logo. For example, when you see an image of an apple with a little bite out of it, you know it means Apple, the company. Dream images as symbols are more complex, expansive, fluid, more like poetry through which meaning is communicated by metaphor, analogy, synecdoche (where one aspect stands for the whole thing), pun, or other loose reference.

Interpreting dreams is like unlocking a secret code and completing a jigsaw puzzle all at the same time. When you get there, a warm feeling will pour through you. It will be an important "aha" moment, and you will feel the mystery and magic of the dream world come alive.

HOW TO INTERPRET YOUR DREAMS

Interpretation is based on the idea of translating a language of images into the language of words and meaning. Sometimes words are part of a dream—perhaps as part of a conversation, or a note or letter, or a voice telling you what to do next—but, mostly, dreams are made up of pictures, action, drama, and movement.

To take you through the process of dream interpretation, here are some basic steps:

1. Find the central image of the dream. It could be an object or person, a relationship, an emotion, an action, or something else.

2. Name the key emotion of the dream.

3. Identify the most important, unique, or defining characteristics of the central image.

4. Deepen the meaning by giving it a personal context. Consider how you relate to that image and its characteristics based on your life experience.

5. Imagine laying out the pieces of what you've discovered like a puzzle. You may need to shift, juggle, and analyze them until they come together to form a meaningful picture.

Here's an example of how you can put these steps into action. Let's imagine you had the following dream:

I drove my car to the farmers' market and bought some beets.

Find the central image. The place to start is with the individual images. Of the many objects, characters, or actions that may appear in a dream, often, one stands out. There are many images in this small dream: I, the car, the farmers' market, and the beets. Actions are also images, and there are two here—driving and buying. You could begin with any of the images, but the central one is *buying the beets*. You want to know—what is the deeper meaning of the dream?

It's easy to dismiss the dream by saying to yourself, "Oh, I had this dream because I was grocery shopping yesterday and saw some beets." Even if that is true, your eyes fell on thousands of objects that your dreaming self could have seized upon, but *beets* are what the dream maker chose. Trust your dream maker to have selected specific images because they hold special meaning for you.

Identify the key emotion. Take yourself back into your dream. What were you feeling? If you were feeling more than one emotion, what was the strongest or most lasting one? See if you can let that emotion wake up as you record your dream and think about it. In this dream, you were feeling happy.

Identify the most important characteristics of the central image. Once you've identified a particular image, the first step in interpreting the image is to wonder about its common or universal traits. This will help you grasp the symbolic meaning of the image. So, now, you're curious—why beets?

What is unique about beets and common to everyone, not just you? Beets are extremely nutritious, inexpensive, and totally consumable—you can eat both the root and the leaves. They are an important antioxidant and super healthy for you. They are red or yellow, colorful, and grow underground.

So, the dream is saying you acquired something healthy, nutritious, and totally available to you to digest and benefit from. It grows in the dark (maybe grows in the unconscious?); it is a root vegetable (maybe root referring to place of origin?).

Add your personal connection. Once you figure out the common and universal meaning of beets, add your experience or connection to the item.

Let's say, during childhood, you hated beets but your mother forced you to eat them. The dream is suggesting something healthy and good for you with an association to your mother. You add another piece: Once, after being forced to eat beets, you got sick all over the kitchen table. The dream is pointing to you rejecting your mother's food, even though it might have been good for you.

Now, put some of the pieces together. Does the feeling in the dream match the remembered feeling? How do the actions and feelings of the dream relate to your association?

It appears that something you are currently acquiring, something with an emotional past, has changed. You are getting something very good for you that you used to reject. In childhood, you rejected your mother's forced nutritional offering, but the dream shows an inner attitude has changed.

It's important, at this point, to jot down a few notes about what is going on in your waking life so you can connect the meaning of the dream to what is happening. Let's say you just had a job interview a day or so before having this dream. The message might be warning you not to behave as you did as a child. It shows you acquiring for yourself what your mother offered—something healthy. The dream might be saying you have done something good for yourself, but you aren't aware of it yet. You are growing "underground"—that is, there is growth, but you don't see it yet.

Dreams are amazingly smart. They have a sense of humor and they are great punsters. So, with the beet dream—what are the other meanings of *beet*? Maybe beats? Did I get some new beats, as in rhythm, or as in a routine, like every police officer has a beat? Or did I get hurt, as in, I got some beats, meaning someone hit me?

Put together the puzzle. Now comes the fun. You slide these possible meanings around trying to connect them to what happened recently, to see where your associations to "beets" take you.

In the following pages, you'll find descriptions of some images that occur frequently in dreams. When you have a dream image, before turning there to see what is written about your dream image, try to extract the common meaning for yourself. Gradually, you'll build up interpretation skills and increase the ease with which you approach the images. Once you give yourself a chance to work on the symbol, refer to this book to amplify the image further.

In addition to figuring out the meaning, you'll want to think about what aspect of life your dream points toward. Sometimes dreams report on interpersonal relationships by giving you an additional perspective on what is going on in your life. Earlier, I told you about the dream I had where the woman told me I had moved into a slum. The dream maker saw something I wasn't ready yet to take in.

Another layer of meaning is internal. A dream can give you information about how different parts of yourself are working with one another. For example, if you dream about an argument between your mother and you, it could point to something between the two of you that is just below the surface, or it could be that the "mothering" part of you is in conflict with another part of you. Sometimes, when you really nail down the meaning of a dream, both may be true.

THE DREAM DICTIONARY: COMMON SIGNS, SYMBOLS, AND MEANINGS

The study of symbols never ends. All cultures have systems of symbols—sometimes meanings are consistent across cultures and, other times, meanings vary. For example, the egg as a symbol of the beginning is universal, whereas the cross varies in its symbolism. In Christianity, it represents the crucifixion; in Chinese, it represents the number 10; and the Celtic cross stands for unification of all things. As you learn about the universal meaning and archetypal aspect of the symbols occurring in your dreams, you'll gain valuable insight into the messages and, in time, develop your personal symbolism. An excellent way to expand your knowledge is to study symbol systems such as astrology, tarot, the *I Ching*, and mythologies and religions of the world.

Settings, Environments, and Locations

Locations often provide the context for the dream, particularly locations of the natural world. They give us clues about where we are in our life's journey and are symbolic of the state of our internal world.

Beach and shoreline—This is the mysterious boundary between land and water. Always shifting, but also always there, this boundary has ambivalent symbolic meaning. The beach is a place where you can play, relax, picnic, and swim. But build your house too close to the shoreline and you may experience a disaster. Like the ocean, the shoreline can be the location of elemental disaster as well as carefree natural fun. Pay attention to the level of turbulence, because this will give you clues about the inner state of your emotions.

Bridge and tunnel—Both structures are ways of traversing natural barriers or obstacles. A bridge is an obvious connector of two points. But, when you think more deeply about a bridge, it is humankind's creation that defies a natural boundary. Being that the bridge is so defiant of nature, it is also a risky structure subject to collapse. Tunnels are like bridges but, instead of going over ground, they go underground. The important distinction in a dream would be that a tunnel suggests something unseen—it's a more deeply unconscious symbol.

Church or temple—As a place of worship, a church or temple makes an obvious connection to spiritual life. In a dream, it may represent the pathway to a more deeply-felt spiritual reality. Sometimes spiritual paths open up in contexts that don't appear "spiritual." For example, if you dream that you go into a temple and find tables set up for painting, you might want to try art as a way to deepen spiritual connections.

Crossroad or intersection—The crossroad is a liminal, or in-between, space. If you think about a road, the intersection is a positive opportunity because you can change direction, but is also dangerous because it's a place where a collision is more likely to occur. Most often, the crossroads shows up when you are making a big change, moving forward in your life, tempting you back to the familiar. When the crossroad or intersection shows up in the dream, be careful about the decision you've made. If you can stick to your guns, you'll move ahead even though there is a pull to retreat.

Forest—The forest is traditionally a dangerous place in fairy tales. Children who go off in the forest meet big challenges. Going into the forest or woods signifies a challenge or difficult situation, one that will be scary, but will test your cleverness, resilience, and strength.

House—The house that appears in your dream may be a house that is familiar to you. A childhood home is a common dream location. Most of us spend much of our lives working on issues that originate from childhood. The appearance of that house suggests that you go back and think about what happened based on the clues the dream provides. Whatever house you imagine, generally, it represents the psychological space in which you live.

Kitchen—The kitchen is the heart of the home, the place where nourishment is prepared and family gathers. It represents the alchemical vessel where transformation occurs by way of the different processes that happen there—chopping, mixing, heating, and cooling. Kitchen implements are important dream images, too.

Moon—Unlike the Sun, the Moon has no light of its own, only reflected light. The Moon may suggest the energy of being a satellite around a more powerful entity. The Moon, symbolically, carries the constancy of change. The New Moon, usually, is a time of beginning, whereas the Full Moon is a period of completion and letting go. The Moon is associated with silver.

Mountain—The mountain is strong, steady, and immutable. Relating to a mountain requires you to either go around it or put on hiking boots and get ready for a strenuous climb. A mountain may represent an important obstacle or challenge you can't avoid. Because, most often, you don't dream that you ARE the mountain, it also means there is some tremendous natural strength or stillness you need to tap.

Ocean—One of the most common symbolic features that appears in dreams, the ocean is an image of a vast unknown world. As the source of all life, it is often taken as an image of the unconscious itself, a huge psychic space. Pay attention to what the ocean is doing in your dream. It can be gentle or turbulent and threatening to overwhelm. The state of the ocean will tell you about the state of the deep unconscious within you. When it roils, reflect on your inner storms.

Sky and outer space—Many religions of the world imagine heaven as being located in the sky. As a symbol of the infinite, the sky and outer space can mean limitless possibilities. Floating in outer space, however, can indicate you are ungrounded and dangerously untethered.

Star—The star is a standout, a guiding light. Star power wants you to shine and take your place in the spotlight. The star is an elemental factor that helps you find your way, like the ancients who navigated using the constellations. We also have the expression "it's in the stars," meaning something is fated. Gold stars are praise for accomplishments.

Sun and light—Providing the warmth we need for life to exist, and the star at the center of our solar system, the Sun is a symbol of power, warmth, and light. Bringing an issue into the light, turning on a light in a dark room, and sunrise are all images of emerging consciousness. Other images that share this domain of meaning, each with a slightly different slant, include candles, flashlights, headlights, and campfires. The Sun is associated with the metal gold.

People and Relationships

RELATIVES AND FAMILY

When a dream brings a family member, it's one of the most poignant cases that illustrates how dreams are multilayered—that is, focused on the interpersonal layer and the internal layer. The first layer: Is there anything you need to consider in your relationship with this person? Why might your dream maker bring this person to the dream in this way? On the internal layer, think about this figure symbolically. What do you think this person stands for? What are this person's most significant qualities? How might your dream maker be using this person to stand for a quality you need to embrace? The dream may illustrate a need for more connection with a quality rather than a specific person.

In addition, all family figures have an archetypal significance. For example, the mother might be your mother, but it could also be pointing to the archetypal Great Mother. Sometimes when you really come to understand a dream deeply, you may find that different layers have important meaning at the same time. It isn't either/or.

Baby—Babies appear frequently in dreams, representing new life. The baby's age is important because it may help you recognize the project or situation the dream is focused on. Whatever the age of the baby, count back to its "birth" to see what might have begun then. Babies who are shrinking or shriveling indicate neglect of something important.

Brother and sister—Just like the partner, the sibling may relate to an issue between you and that person. Beyond that, in our culture, there are still gender stereotypes. There are behaviors and qualities that are culturally or socially more acceptable to one gender than the other. Not that it is correct, or should be this way, but gender expectations and unspoken parameters continue to shape social behavior. For this reason, sometimes a sibling of the opposite sex will come into a dream exhibiting a trait the dreamer wasn't able to integrate into the personality because it felt too masculine or too feminine. When this happens, it's often a clue it's time to expand the sense of self to include this trait.

Daughter—When a daughter appears in a dream, particularly in the dream of a woman (even if she has no children), the daughter often represents a revitalizing energy. Like Persephone, the Greek goddess of spring, the daughter who appears in a dream may be the image of the energy that brings something back to life. The archetypal daughter is also connected to the theme of devotion. For a woman, the daughter may represent an emerging or growing aspect of her personality, or a spark of vitality.

Father—The father may reference your parent and indicate you are working through issues with them. The archetypal father represents power, authority, and the law. The archetypal father is also the one who inseminates and initiates the cycle of new life. Ra, the Sun god of ancient Egypt, created life from his sweat and tears. Sometimes body fluids appear in a dream—semen, sweat, tears. When they do, those fluids may have the power to start growth just like Ra's sweat and tears in myth.

Grandparents and ancestors—Grandparents and ancestors represent the family's legacy, whether they are alive or have passed on. Pay attention to the context around them because it may give you clues as to what needs to become more conscious or more valued from the past. When these figures come into your dream, try to determine what are the gifts of your family's legacy, and what baggage you might carry emanating from these past generations. Sometimes pains of past generations are successfully healed in the present and prevented from carrying forward to current or future generations.

Lover—In a dream, the lover represents a bond or irresistible attraction to a particular set of traits or characteristics. What is it about the lover in your dream that draws you? When you fall in love, the lover becomes irresistible because you experience something within you that you can't access by yourself. Like Sleeping Beauty, the lover wakes up a wonderful part of you. In a dream, just as in your awake life, ask yourself, "What does the lover wake up in me?"

Mother—Mothers are probably one of the most common characters to show up in dreams. Many of us spend years coming to terms with our relationship with our mothers. At the first level of meaning, think about the dream actually being about the person who is your mother. Beyond that, the image of "mother" may mean the source or the ground from which you emerged. The mother is also often an image that represents your physical body, your "home." The sign of the zodiac associated with the mother, the home, and all things maternal is Cancer. I have seen quite a few dreams in which a reference to "cancer" was actually pointing to mothering. For example, a woman who dreamed she had been diagnosed with cancer discovered that, not the disease, but too much mothering was making her sick.

Partner, wife, or husband—Your life partner inevitably will show up often in your dreams. Sometimes it's your way of working through snags in the relationship. Sometimes it's calling your attention to a problem that you and/or your partner are unconsciously avoiding. When your real-life partner is in your dream, pay attention to what the dream is pointing out. A stranger who is your partner in a dream often represents some trait or characteristic that is far away from awareness.

Son—Apart from the actual relative, the son is an image of how the future carries on. In Western culture, traditionally, the family name is carried into the future by the son; while that is changing, the archetypal meaning points in that direction. The son is associated with the yang principle—active, outgoing, penetrating, noisy. The son may represent active, outgoing qualities that exist in potential for the future. Like the daughter to the mother, the son may represent an emerging or growing aspect of a man's personality.

PROFESSIONS

When a figure from a specific profession appears, think about the main function of that profession and what you might need. For example, a physician and nurse are medical and health care professionals, but the physician is an interventionist whereas the nurse is a caretaker. Here are a few significant professions that can appear in dreams.

Chauffeur or taxi driver—The chauffeur will take you on a relatively short trip, but in style, and the ride will be cushy. The taxi driver is a more regular form of chauffeur, but the "meter is running." You will always want to know if it was necessary for you to have a "driver" in this dream situation. If not, ask why.

Famous iconic figures—Rock stars, movie icons, politicians, and other similar figures show up often in dreams. Think about what that figure stands for. It's likely you need to incorporate some of that energy into your life.

Firefighter or EMT—When a firefighter or EMT shows up in your dream, think emergency. Your unconscious is trying to communicate that something happening in your real life needs immediate attention.

Head of state or president—As the head officer of any government, social organization, or institution, the head, whether president, king or queen, or prime minister, represents a ruling or governing principle. This figure often symbolizes the values around which you organize your life and will shine a light on that.

Priest or priestess—As a figure, not only does the priest or priestess officiate over religious ceremonies, they also bridge or connect realms, the seen and unseen, the sacred and profane, the spiritual and material. This figure is an agent of transformation. If you have a religious affiliation, think about what that means to you. If you don't, then the arrival of this figure may be pointing you in the direction of developing a spiritual value by turning toward an established faith community or developing a faith-based practice on your own.

Therapist—If you are in therapy, it's always a good idea to report a dream about your therapist to that person. Therapists attend to various parts of us—physical therapy, psychotherapy, and occupational therapy are the most frequent. Dreams about your therapy or therapist may represent how the therapy is going, or may clue you in to something that needs to be addressed. For example, if you dream there is a leak in your therapist's office, you may be worried about confidentiality.

Animals

Animals, frequent visitors to dream life, represent instincts or specific natural energies. When you work with dream animals, ask yourself why your dream maker might have chosen this particular animal. Each has unique characteristics and the more you connect to these unique attributes, the more deeply you can understand your dream. You will also notice certain animals show up in multiples, such as flocks of birds, schools of fish, packs of dogs, pods of whales, colonies of bees, etc. When the animals are numerous in this way, think about the power of the particular species being intensified. Among certain animals, the appearance of the group rather than the individual animal emphasizes the social aspect of that species. For example, a single bee may represent a creature that flits about gathering nectar, whereas a hive of bees represents a community that works together to sustain itself.

Bear—The bear is a potent totem animal. Because it hibernates, the bear has the capacity to regulate its metabolism. Often, a bear appears when a person is about to slip into a depression—not necessarily a pathological depression, but the kind of depression that precedes a creative burst. The bear is an image of a powerful mothering instinct. It is also the symbol for California and Russia.

Cat—Cats are natural predators; though domesticated, they are so close to their primitive roots that most house cats, if they had to, could revert to the wild and survive. In its domesticated capacity, the cat protects boundaries and prevents vermin and other pests from invading. In this way, the cat is to the house what immune system T cells are to the body—pouncing on invaders. Sick or dying cats in a dream sometimes indicate a flagging immune system. A rich symbol, there are many meanings to the cat. When a cat appears, try on a number of meanings: Think quiet and stealth; think "catty."

Crocodile and alligator—These two creatures are often confused with one another; however, the crocodile is much more dangerous than the alligator. The alligator is actually a timid creature that is naturally fearful of humans. The croc, on the other hand, is bad-tempered and likely to attack. Both guard their eggs, and lovingly guide the babies into the water. Only minutes after performing this maternal gesture, they will gobble up their offspring if they don't swim away fast enough. If one of these creatures appears in your dream, think about the dangerous, big mouth and the ambivalent mothering.

Deer—With its antlers reaching toward the sky, the deer is a symbol of spiritual authority. With its agile feet firmly on the ground and its antlers lifting skyward, the deer is often a totem animal for the shaman, the one in the tribe or culture who bridges between the everyday world of the community and the unseen spirit realm. Yearly, the deer's antlers fall off and grow back, so, like the snake that sheds its skin, the deer is a symbol of regeneration. It can also represent grace, elegance, and gentleness. Their only defense is to flee.

Dog—Humankind's best friend, the dog, is the ultimate symbol of companionship and loyalty. Because a dog is often the companion of a witch, it also carries a meaning of being highly intuitive. Sometimes dogs know more about you than you know about yourself. When a dog comes to you in a dream, welcome the loyalty, companionship, and insight it brings.

Dolphin—The mythology around the dolphin is rich and universal from culture to culture. It is one of the few animals known to play and, like the whale, is a mammal at home in the sea. The dolphin is protective of other dolphins, and of swimmers, sometimes bumping a drowning person to the surface, or swimming circles around a swimmer in danger of a shark attack. It is thought to be a friend to sailors; a dolphin is a good omen when following a boat and, in dreams, you are sailing the waters of the unconscious. So, if a dolphin should grace your dream, consider it a fortuitous sign.

Frog and toad—Very similar in nature, the frog has a slimy, moist skin, whereas the toad has a dry, bumpy one. In ancient Egyptian mythology, the frog was a symbol of fertility because frogs emerged from the dark sludge of the Nile after it flooded in spring. The frog or toad has ambivalent meaning, both regenerative and poisonous. If a frog or toad comes to you in a dream, it might signify some new life is about to emerge from a dark place. Alternately, it could point to dark, witchy energy (like intuition, stealth, or magic) that wants to use these skills to concoct a hex or spell to make your wish come true.

Hippopotamus—Literally, meaning "horse of the river," the hippo lives near rivers in Africa. The hippo actually walks along the bottom of the river and, in this way, stamps down vegetation, making the animal a helper who keeps the river flowing. As a mythical figure in Egypt, Taurt, the hippo goddess, presided over childbirth; she opened the channel. A little bit like the plumber, if a hippo shows up in a dream, she's there to open some channel that might be blocked. The other interesting thing about the hippopotamus is that it is very thick-skinned, yet its skin is vulnerable.

Horse—The horse is a highly intuitive animal that "reads" its rider in precise and accurate ways. It knows what you are thinking and feeling because it has "horse sense." It is also imaged as a magical animal that can talk and have visions. The horse is the instinct of power that will carry you far and give you freedom. Because it is ridden between the legs, it can also be a symbol of sexual power and energy. If the horse is a mare, it may represent the mother or a female body.

Lion—The king of the jungle, the lion, appears often in dreams. The lion is a solar animal, meaning it hunts and is active during the day. From a psychological point of view, this means the light of consciousness. The lion is also a communal animal, living in a pride for the most part. The female lion, identified without the massive mane of the male, is the worker of the pride. Her role as provider shows up in women's dreams when a woman is coming into her own power in the world. Because of its association with "pride," when lions appear, think about feeling pride, or if it appears in a negative light, being too prideful.

Monkey and ape—Our most closely related primates, monkeys and apes are highly social and community oriented. When meditating, the mind often jumps from one thing to another—this is referred to as "monkey mind." That lack of focus and jumping-around energy can be symbolized by a monkey in a dream. The monkey can also be a trickster figure.

Mouse and rat—A mouse is a small, hardy animal with an extraordinary ability to survive extremes in temperature and scarcities of food. The rat, much larger, carries more negative connotation as a spreader of disease. The rat will infest and proliferate wherever it finds food and shelter. In the English language, the expression, "Rats!" essentially means, "Oh no!" A "rat" is often the idiomatic term for someone who betrays another.

Rabbit—Known for its ability to reproduce, the rabbit is a symbol of fertility and prolific production. Rabbits have no real defense system. When terrified, they freeze and play dead. If a rabbit appears in your dream while you are in a tough situation, it may be pointing to being defenseless. Alternatively, the rabbit's foot is a symbol of good luck.

Shark—Sharks pop up in dreams with surprising frequency. One of the most important things about sharks is that they need to keep moving forward. If a shark is pursuing you in a dream, think about a place in your life where you are stuck or dragging your heels. Shark imagery is a powerful antidote for procrastination.

Snake—The snake is a universally terrifying creature. Because the snake sheds its skin, it's also a symbol of renewal and regeneration. As a symbol, the snake curls around the caduceus, symbol of the medical profession; the rod of Asclepius; as well as the double snake curled around the staff of Hermes, the messenger god. Snake venom can be both toxic and healing. A snakebite often signifies the beginning of a healing cycle.

Tiger—Like the lion, the tiger is a stunning image of powerful animal instinct. Because the tiger is mostly a solitary animal, the appearance of a tiger in your dream is likely to encourage you to embody powerful instincts on your own rather than in a group or community.

Wolf—The wolf lives in a social order, mating for life. Because it travels and hunts in a pack, it is highly organized for predatory purposes. Many cultures project evil and destructiveness on the wolf, such as werewolves. The wolf appears in many metaphoric expressions, such as "hungry as a wolf" and "crying wolf." When a wolf appears in your dream, it is a powerful image of focused, abiding power. Having been near extinction in North America and making a comeback, it may represent the return of powerful energy for you.

Objects

When you find an object in a dream, think about how that object is used, what it does, how it functions, and how it is unique. Dream images are surprisingly specific, so pay attention to its particularity.

Computer—Today computers, mobile phones, and all sorts of technological devices are showing up in dreams. The computer may represent your mind, memory, or mental processing strategies. The mobile phone is a connective device, your way of reaching the people you care about or need to contact. In a dream, you can think about them specifically, but also wonder what they represent symbolically.

Gun—Guns almost always appear in dreams as potent instruments of aggression. The one who carries the gun in the dream is displaying the power of life and death.

Jewelry and ring—Jewelry always represents a precious and valuable asset of enduring and permanent value, often symbolically connected to the person who gave the piece. The ring, in particular, because of its circle shape, stands for enduring, endless commitment.

Knife—Knives cover an array of symbolic meanings. Paring knives are used to cut large things into smaller, digestible pieces. Jackknives and daggers are used to harm another person. Penknives, favored by adolescents, are used to whittle small objects. When a knife is severing objects, it can be the instrument of liberation, freeing you from whatever binds or constrains you.

Poison—Ingesting poison in a dream may point to the dreamer's struggle with self-harmful behaviors or attitudes. In a dream, what appears to be poison may actually be a healing substance, like snake venom, which is both toxic and healing.

Rope—A common object used to lash things together, the rope has ambivalent meaning in a dream. "Tying the knot" is a euphemism for marriage, or the commitment to a lasting relationship. Being "tied up in knots" means to be confused, worried, or paralyzed. The rope can be an image of securing safety, like anchoring, or involuntary control, like tying up the dog, so the meaning depends on how the rope appears in a dream.

Tears—The body's "rain," tears have healing, growth-promoting power. If they begin in a dream, be grateful and think about finding a way to shed them when you are awake.

Teeth—Teeth falling out is one of the most common anxiety dreams. There are a wide range of possibilities for this scenario—from terrible fear of loss to arrival of a new friend. Here's another possibility: Our teeth are the "gate" to the inner world. Biting is our earliest ability to inflict harm or hurt on another person, a primary line of defense. You might wonder if this dream image means you are losing your first line of defense, and thus, feel threatened on a primary or primitive level.

Wallet—A frequent dream object, the wallet is a container of important aspects of identity and simple objects we need daily. Losing a wallet can signify a loss of identity. One thing to keep in mind is that a wallet is only necessary to navigate the outer world. Losing a wallet or not being able to find it may indicate the need for an inner journey rather than an outer one, or it may point to the dreamer needing to secure some piece of identity.

Water—Water appears frequently in dreams. As the basic element of life, it can represent feelings, emotions, or the pulse of life. Floods can indicate becoming emotionally overwhelmed. Leaky roofs or houses suggest something needs to be contained, perhaps confidentiality or that a private matter isn't safe. Plumbing problems usually have to do with emotions not flowing smoothly or being jammed up. Aridity, or too much dryness, may indicate a lack of feeling, or the need for a good cry. Tears, a form of water, are nature's healing elixir.

Numbers and Colors

NUMBERS

Numbers appear frequently in dreams. They may appear as the age of a person, the number of years, or the number of objects. Especially in animals, the multiples amplify the power of the individual animal. When the number refers to an age, think about what happened to you at that time, or that many years ago.

In dreams, a pair, twins, or doubling is a very important pattern that announces a new energy coming alive in the psyche. For example, in a dream, if a person notices two new cars in the garage, it is likely the dream is announcing a new potential for navigating the outer world.

COLORS

Colors appear naturally in the world around us. Some people dream in black and white, but sometimes even a person who has become blind will dream in color. Pay attention to the color in your dreams, particularly if the image appears in an unusual color, one that is not its natural color.

Black—The color of mourning, death, and the night, black rules many things you fear—loss, absence, and infinite emptiness. Alternatively, black is stylish, sophisticated, and formal, as in a "black-tie" affair. Depending on culture, racial backgrounds, and identity, black and its counterpart, white, will have different meanings.

Blue—Blue, the soothing, calm color of a clear sky or pool of water, carries the sense of vastness, serenity, and clarity. Its temperature is cool. In spite of the comforting aspects of the color, becoming "blue" is often a sign of depression. The unconscious plays with words like this. For example, if I am wearing blue jeans, it may be a pun for blue genes, meaning I am genetically inclined toward depression. Other expressions, such as "out of the blue" or "once in a blue moon," suggest sudden or rare occurrences. In Western culture, blue is also the color associated with a male baby. Blue is the color of the fifth, or throat, chakra, the portal of voice and freedom.

Brown—Brown is the color of Earth, ground, and nature. Reliable and steady, brown grounds you. Brown eyes are soft and melt your heart. Chocolate is sometimes felt as a turn-to substitute for love. Brown skin may indicate exposure to sunlight, or point to a cultural or racial meaning.

Green—The color of nature is soothing and represents growth, development, and hope. Green can indicate not yet ripe or immature, or green with envy. The color rules the fourth, or heart, chakra, which is associated with love and self-acceptance.

Purple—Purple is the color of royalty and nobility, mystery, magic, intoxicating grapes, and fragrant lilacs. Purple is the color of the sixth, or the third eye, chakra, the seat of intuition and sense of purpose.

Red—Red is the color of blood, passion, rage, and heat and a color that belongs to the devil. Turning red can signify terrible embarrassment or fury. Red roses, red lips, and the red-light district signify the life force *eros* and sexuality. And don't forget a red light means STOP. In healing, red is associated with the first, or root, chakra, which governs the sense of trust, belonging, and safety.

White—White is the color of archetypal purity and innocence, worn by brides for marriage and babies for baptism. When an object appears white, particularly if it is not usually white, pay special attention to it. The white object often announces a transformation—something powerful is on the horizon for you. Often, the transformation is emotional, psychological, and spiritual, a deep and meaningful change. White is also the color of the seventh, or crown, chakra (sometimes colored purple), the portal through which you connect to the divine.

Yellow—Yellow is both the warm color of sunshine and the color of cowardice. Yellowing can indicate aging, becoming decrepit, and needing refreshment. Often, yellow is associated with joy and expansiveness. It is connected to the third, or solar plexus, chakra in healing traditions—the portal of personal power and self-confidence. A yellow light often signifies caution. Buses and taxis are often yellow so they can be noticed easily.

Modes of Transportation

All forms of transportation appear with surprising frequency in dreams. They tell you about methods of getting around—that is, how you navigate your world. They often represent coping strategies, skills, abilities, and strengths.

Airplane, helicopter, and rocket—All are equipped to take you long distances in short periods of time. The airplane, unless you are a pilot, indicates letting someone else be in control of getting you where you want to go. The difference with a helicopter is that it can get into places often otherwise inaccessible and is agile and can make quick, sharp turns, which an airplane can't. The rocket can take you right out of this world.

Bicycle—The bike gets you where you want to go, but requires effort—and lots of it. It is a beautiful image in a dream because it tells you that you are both the driver and the energy source.

Riding a bicycle in a dream is a powerful symbolic reflection of your autonomy, self-directedness, and energy.

Boat—When you think about the ocean or bodies of water as representative of the unconscious, a boat is the symbolic means of navigating the unconscious.

Bus—Buses follow prescribed routes rather than individual ones. A bus may not take you directly to your destination; it may get you in the general area, after which you will have to supply additional effort to reach your destination. In general, a bus is a thrifty means of transportation but one that will take longer than other means. The school bus may point back to earlier childhood experiences.

Car—The car is a personal means of transportation that allows you to make an individual journey along a route you choose. It represents the ordinary way you get around your world (if you live in a place where you drive daily). When your dream shows you driving someone else's car, think about whether you are functioning in a way that is authentic to your personality, or whether the dream is trying to show you have taken on someone else's style.

Train, tram, and cable car—The key to the symbolic meaning of these modes of transportation is that their path is wedded to a rail or cable. This means that, even more than a bus, the train and these other means of transportation are rigidly held to a pre-determined path from which they cannot deviate. If you dream about a train ride when you begin a new job, you can be sure you will be required to follow very specific pre-determined patterns.

Walking and running—These are our most basic means of transportation; self-directed, and, even when at great speed, still slow and mostly limited to relatively short distances. Dreams about walking and running, particularly when you dream you are in danger, or trying to get away from a malevolent threat, symbolically highlight your vulnerability and lack of support in the face of a difficult situation.

Experiences

Experiences that occur in dreams, rather than having symbolic meaning, often represent exactly what they are. What matters is what the experience does to the dreamer. Rather than seek a symbolic meaning, it is worth wondering why the dream maker would want the dreamer to have this experience. There is also value in considering the dreamer's experience from the point of view of other characters of the dream. For example, let's say a 12-year-old boy comes in and scribbles on an important project. With a dream like this, you could ask yourself—does my project need a little of that youthful energy?

Abandonment—Sometimes in a dream, the dreamer feels abandoned. Abandonment is a feeling state in which ties that once connected you become severed, leaving you untethered and feeling alone. Also implicit in the theme of abandonment is the state of being orphaned—being alone without others to care for you. Often, in dreams, the experience of being abandoned is an early step in the individuation process, a stage where you feel alone, bereft, and on your own.

Being chased—A common nightmare theme, being pursued by a malevolent other or force provokes an intense effort to escape.

Sometimes paralysis sets in and, in spite of wanting to move, you feel paralyzed. You might even try to scream, but nothing comes out. This nightmare might be a clue about something with which you don't feel able to cope; something that feels like it might overwhelm you, or something so powerful, in the face of which you feel utterly inadequate.

Birth—Giving birth, or the arrival of an infant child or baby animal, signals the inception of a new energy, project, issue, or other psychological situation. It is almost always the harbinger of something positive emerging in the psyche. When the infant or baby animal is frail, it indicates the need for special care and nurturance. If the baby or animal is withering away, some new energy is in danger of fizzling out. Pay special attention to birth and new beginnings, because, just like an infant, it needs your nurturing attention.

Death—Dreaming of a death seldom means a physical death. Like the Death card of the tarot, symbolically, death announces an ending, a necessary phase that precedes the emergence of something new. It can signify putting an issue, relationship, or situation to rest. If you are dying in your dream, some aspect of your conscious identity is being shed. Sometimes in a dream, a ghost appears. The ghost often represents some issue that has not been put to rest but needs attention to be put behind you.

Discovery—This theme is almost magical in a dream. The discovery experience is an opening of new territory, whether a new object, new person, new room in your house, etc. All these announce expansion and growth of your psyche and psychological space.

Falling—The experience of falling is a loss of control and the loss of stable ground under your feet. Dreams of falling occur when a person feels vulnerable and when predictable circumstances begin to change. This can be a good sign of new energy coming in, which makes you feel wobbly—or it can be a sign your trusted patterns aren't working anymore.

Flying—Most people who experience flying in dreams love the feeling and find it exhilarating. Defying one of the basic laws of nature, gravity, gives you an inflated sense of self. Sometimes flying offers a new perspective, where you get a "bird's-eye view" and are able to take in a much wider grasp of a situation. Sometimes you dream of flying because you're avoiding conflict by rising up into your head to escape emotions. When you think about your flying dream and its relationship to your real-life situation, you may be able to figure out if the flying dream is supporting you or warning you. Sometimes in a dream, both meanings are valid at the same time.

Late arrival—Like losing teeth, this is a common dream theme. The experience of a late arrival may be your dream maker's way of helping you become aware that time is marching on. Perhaps there are openings just right for you to take certain actions, and the dream warns not to miss the boat.

Loss—Sometimes when a person dreams about a loss, especially a real loss, the dream helps a person process grief. Another meaning of loss in a dream may point to a loss necessary to grow and move on. For example, a woman preparing to file for divorce dreamed she lost her wedding ring. When a loss comes up in your dream, ask yourself whether you are hanging on to something that you need to let go of. What part of you is experiencing the loss? Like the snake that loses its skin or the stag that loses its antlers, loss can be a necessary precursor to growth.

Marriage and divorce—Occasionally, these experiences coincide with what is happening in your real outer life. Both are stressful times and can be represented in dreams as you work through the many complicated emotions connected to either event. Symbolically, marriage and divorce are about elements of personality or energies of life joining or separating. In your dream, if you are marrying a stranger, pay attention to the details. What traits could your psyche want you to embrace more intimately?

Unpreparedness—Just like the late arrival, this theme in your dream may be trying to get your attention so you are adequately prepared to take action. Most of us have had the dream of taking an exam for which we were unprepared. Ask yourself if you are ready for what is coming down the pike. Is there some detail of life you neglect? Do you need anything or need to develop the skills to move ahead?

Natural Phenomena

Occurrences in the natural environment point to intrinsic states of the psyche. Emotions, rhythms of energy, vitality, and inner states are like weather in that they are variable, unpredictable, and autonomous. When a dream shows unfavorable climate, it is wise to take note. This is not pathological or problematic. The timing may simply need to be revised in accord with the inner "weather," so you can move forward when the natural climate is more favorable. If you have had an experience of the natural phenomenon, it may be your psyche's way of working through what you felt during that event.

Earthquake—Earthquakes occur when tectonic plates deep within Earth rub against each other, causing the ground under your feet to tremble. Minor or major, an earthquake in a dream tells you something in your grounding is shifting, or that two major aspects of personality are rubbing against each other. The dream earthquake often indicates deep changes beginning to rumble.

Fire—Fires in dreams can mean many things. Fire may indicate anger, rage, passion, or desire. Fire is also a transformative element or energy, one the alchemists viewed as necessary to turn one substance into another. Fire produces the warmth we all need to feel safe. Because fire can decimate structures, and even forests, when fire appears in a dream, some out-of-control emotion is near eruption. Wildfires in your dream may be provoked by your fear of harm being done to the environment.

Rain—Our natural source of irrigation, rain is necessary for life and, particularly, for initiating growth. Where there is a dearth of water, arid land and deserts become places of little growth. Often, in dreams, rain is connected to emotions, especially tears, which, when they fall, moisten the soil of the personality, soften frozen defenses, and make way for deep growth and transformation.

Rainbow—The rainbow promises hope for the future. Just as we are happy to see a rainbow at the end of a storm, symbolically, the rainbow signifies the end of a perilous time. In Greek mythology, the goddess Iris was a messenger who, sometimes, appeared as the rainbow. Sometimes in dreams, this positive rainbow message appears as the iris flower. The interesting thing is that this kind of archetypal image can appear even though you are unaware of its meaning.

Sunset and sunrise—Both are liminal times—that is, moments of transition from light to dark and dark to light. Likewise, dreams including this element of change are harbingers of things on the cusp of change.

Thunderstorm—Lightning bolts and thunder belong to Zeus, the head Olympian god of Greek mythology. He wielded his power by striking with lightning, so, as an image, the thunderstorm carries titanic power. In nature, warm air rising to meet cold air causes thunderstorms; if one occurs in your dream, you might wonder where there is a collision of warmth (love) and cold (indifference).

Volcano—When things are roiling and fuming beneath the surface, volcanoes erupt. A volcano represents one of the most powerful phenomena of nature. It can bring terrible destruction, but it is also how new landmasses form. When a volcano appears in your dream, wonder what threatens to erupt in you. Consider whether a good explosion could forge new territory for you.

Wind—The essence of the symbolism of wind is that we cannot see it, but know its presence by the effect of its action. This unseen power could be your intuition, or even extrasensory perception. In a dream, it could also depict an unseen force manifesting. For example, if you dream a big wind blows in and messes up your desk at work, wonder what unseen force is messing with you—time to put on detective gear to figure out the source of this unseen, powerful effect.

HOW TO KEEP JOURNALING AND LEARNING FROM YOUR DREAMS

By the time you arrive here, you may have spent plenty of time writing down your dreams, thinking about them, and deciphering what they are trying to tell you. Hopefully you have had plenty of fun while learning. I hope you now have developed this practice as a routine. If so, have you discovered your dream rhythm? Can you spot some common personal themes? Have you become awed by the creative part of you that comes alive while you sleep?

Once you have completed this journal, it's time to move into your very own dream-journaling practice. Establish a pattern you can sustain over long periods. If you are a prolific dreamer, you may not have time to work on every dream thoroughly. Try to record each one, but give yourself some guidelines about how often you will really work on a dream. Don't ever make dream journaling an onerous task you dread. Keep it easy.

Your dream maker will nudge you to live as your truest, most authentic self. In working with your dreams, silence your inner critic and give your curiosity and imagination free rein. Try on bits of insight gleaned from your dreams, then track what happens in your dream life. Dreams are responsive to the action you take during waking hours and, often, will deliver feedback quickly. Images like a gift or a welcome visit are comparable to getting a gold star for your good work. Watch for them.

The most important thought I would like to leave with you is, your dreams are your very own creative endeavor. You are much more inventive, original, and talented than you ever imagined. Add the creativity of your dreams to your treasury of self-esteem. Your dreams hold so much potential. Stay connected to them.

Resources

BOOKS

Barrett, Deirdre, and Patrick McNamara. *Encyclopedia of Sleep and Dreams*. Santa Barbara, California: Greenwood, 2012.

Morris, Jill. *The Dream Workbook*. Boston: Little Brown and Company, 1985.

Olivetti, Katherine. *Dream Work: 10 Lessons for Understanding Dreams, Kindle edition*. Woodside, California: The Dojo Press, 2016.

Shalit, Erel, and Nancy Swift Furlotti (eds). *The Dream and Its Amplification*. Skiatook, Oklahoma: Fisher King Press, 2013.

Whitmont, Edward, and Sylvia Brinton Perera. *Dreams: A Portal to the Source*. East Sussex, England: Routledge, 1991.

WEBSITES AND BLOGS

ASDreams.org (International Association for the Study of Dreams)
DreamMoods.com
KatherineOlivetti.com

References

Dell'Amore, Christine. "Five Surprising Facts About Daydreaming." *National Geographic*, July 16, 2013. NationalGeographic.com /news/2013/7/130716-daydreaming-science-health-brain.

Jung, C.G. "The Meaning of Psychology for Modern Man." In: *Collected Works of C. G. Jung, Vol. 10. Civilization in Transition*: 2nd ed. Princeton New Jersey: University Press, 1970.

ACKNOWLEDGMENTS

I am deeply grateful to every dreamer who trusted me with a dream. Our collaboration is one of the most significant sources of my knowledge. Friends and colleagues Carol Schaefer, Carol Stacks, Valerie Hone, Terry Iacuso, Beverley Zabriskie, Jeffrey Moulton Benevedes, Linda Ford Blaikie, and Betsy Cohen have supported all aspects of my work. Members of my meditation group, Linda Hennessey Roth, Betsy Rix, Marlene Scherer Stern, Colleen Garrett, Stacy McCarthy, Sandy Shapero, and Bev Abbott, who make magic happen. Writing teachers Gay Walley, Adair Lara, Dani Shapiro, Ellen Sussman, Domi Shoemaker, and Lidia Yuknavitch have honed and encouraged my writing. My sisters Virginia Gildea, Paula Majors, and Barbara Stellway have been enduring support. Above all, I thank my children, Cristina Spencer and Peter Olivetti, their spouses Graham Spencer and Mandi Olivetti, and my grandchildren, Gwendolyn, Cole, Eloise, and August for their love and support, and also for the hope they give me for the future and for believing that the principles of compassion, emotional integrity, and creativity will prevail.

ABOUT THE AUTHOR

Katherine Olivetti is a Jungian analyst and writer. She has lectured and written about dream work, psychological process, creativity, spirituality, and writing and editing. Katherine maintains a private practice in Atherton, California, and a website and blog at www.katherineolivetti.com.

CPSIA information can be obtained
at www.ICGtesting.com
Printed in the USA
JSHW042216230720
6869JS00004B/8